Lullabies

AN ILLUSTRATED SONGBOOK

MUSIC ARRANGED BY RICHARD KAPP

THE METROPOLITAN MUSEUM OF ART
NEW YORK

All the works of art reproduced in this book are from the collection of The Metropolitan Museum of Art.

FRONT COVER DETAILS, READING CLOCKWISE FROM TOP LEFT:
Illustration from *Le Journal de Bébé* by Marie Madeleine Franc-Nohain.
Published by Bernard Grasset, Paris, 1914. The Elisha Whittelsey Collection, The Elisha Whittelsey Fund, 1977 1977.588.1.

Jonathan. Eliot Porter, American, 1901–1990. Gelatin silver print, 1938. Alfred Stieglitz Collection, 1949 49.55.287.
© 1990, Amon Carter Museum, Fort Worth, Texas, Bequest of Eliot Porter.

Illustration from *Vieilles chansons et rondes pour les petits enfants*. Maurice Boutet de Monvel, French, 1851–1913.
Published in Paris. Gift of Mrs. John S. Lamont, 1974 1974.669.

Nurse and Child. Mary Cassatt, American, 1844–1926. Pastel on colored wove paper, mounted on canvas, 1897.
Gift of Mrs. Ralph J. Hines, 1960 60.181.

BACK COVER: *Mother and Child*. Mary Cassatt, American, 1844–1926. Pastel on paper, ca. 1910.
From the Collection of James Stillman, Gift of Dr. Ernest G. Stillman, 1922 22.16.21.

BACK JACKET FLAP: *Portrait of a Child* (Clara B. Fuller). Lucia Fairchild Fuller, American, 1872–1924.
Watercolor on ivory, 1898. Rogers Fund, 1914 14.57.3.

PAGE 1: *Sleeping*. Detail from *A Day in a Child's Life*. Hand-colored wood engraving
after a drawing by Kate Greenaway (British, 1846–1901), 1881. Rogers Fund, 1921 21.36.91.

PAGE 3: Illustration from *Vieilles chansons et rondes pour les petits enfants*. Maurice Boutet de Monvel, French, 1851–1913.
Published in Paris. Gift of Mrs. John S. Lamont, 1974 1974.669.

PAGES 6–7: Illustrations from *Le Journal de Bébé* by Marie Madeleine Franc-Nohain.
Published by Bernard Grasset, Paris, 1914. The Elisha Whittelsey Collection,
The Elisha Whittelsey Fund, 1977 1977.588.1.

Work by Romare Bearden, p. 29: Works of Romare Bearden are licensed by VAGA, New York, NY. Works by Jean Charlot,
pp. 31, 69: Reproduced with the permission of Mrs. Dorothy Zohmah Charlot and the Jean Charlot Estate. Works by Pierre Bonnard,
pp. 36, 39, 48: © 1997 Artists Rights Society (ARS), New York / ADAGP, Paris. Work by Eliot Porter, p. 40 and front cover: © 1990,
Amon Carter Museum, Fort Worth, Texas, Bequest of Eliot Porter. Work by Alma Lavenson, p. 60: Courtesy Alma Lavenson Associates
and Susan Ehrens. Work by Henry Moore, p. 76: Reproduced by permission of the Henry Moore Foundation.

Music for "Dance, Little Baby" and "Matthew, Mark, Luke, and John" composed by Paul Kapp.

Published by The Metropolitan Museum of Art, New York

ISBN 978-1-58839-376-0

Produced by the Department of Special Publications, The Metropolitan Museum of Art
Music arrangements by Richard Kapp
Photography on page 48 by Malcolm Varon, NY
All other photography by The Metropolitan Museum of Art Photograph Studio
Book designed by Barbara Balch

Printed in Italy
K L

THE METROPOLITAN MUSEUM OF ART
1000 Fifth Avenue
New York, NY 10028
212.570.3894
www.metmuseum.org

CONTENTS

INTRODUCTION

The time spent before going to sleep can be one of the sweetest pleasures children and grown-ups share. After the day's busy activities, bedtime is a chance to snuggle together, to recall the events of the day, to create an atmosphere of calm and quiet for the night. Music is often a part of this evening ritual, for lullabies provide a bridge between daytime and dreaming, as they soothe fears, express love, or inspire visions of delights. Gathered here are thirty-seven lullabies, some classic, some less familiar, and all illustrated with works of art from the collections of The Metropolitan Museum of Art.

These songs represent a wide variety of musical styles and traditions, ranging from lullabies by famous composers and poets to simple, anonymous folk songs. Many have a lilting rhythm that mimics a rocking motion. Others have a gentle, murmuring tone that encourages slumber. Also included are livelier songs, for when a child awakens or for babies who respond to music with a definite beat, and a few songs that children can sing to themselves.

The lyrics of these lullabies calm and comfort, some with pleasant imagery of toys and treats, some with reassurances of the parents' love and protection, some with prayers of safekeeping. Of course, tiny babies can't understand the words, anyway, and some of the most effective songs are composed of soothing nonsense syllables: "toora, loora, loora," or "baloo, baleerie."

The songs originated in the British Isles, the American South, Eastern Europe, and other places around the world. The works of art that accompany them similarly come from a wide variety of cultures and times. An ancient Greek sculpture, a Victorian painting, and a twentieth-century photograph all celebrate the innocent contentment of sleep. The tender communication between mothers and children is captured in Mary Cassatt's touching portraits and Gertrude Käsebier's thoughtful photographs, as well as in sculptures from Oceania and ancient Egypt. Views of the family can be found in prints by Pierre Bonnard and Kitagawa Utamaro and a sculpture by Henry Moore. And some of the timeless tools for comforting children are represented by an English seventeenth-century cradle, a Shaker rocking chair, and a Colonial American rattle. Moonlit landscapes, watchful angels, and scenes of nature at rest further evoke tranquillity and quiet.

The songs induce sleepiness, and the images reflect the tenderness and affection that grown-ups feel as they gaze at their now-slumbering children. With soft lashes, dewy cheeks, and damp curls, is there anything sweeter than a sleeping child?

Carolyn Vaughan, Editor

Hush, Little Baby

*This catalogue of gifts—
and Papa's endless willingness
to replace broken toys—has
delighted babies over the years.*

Rocking

The Hatch Family
Eastman Johnson
American, 1824–1906
Oil on canvas, 1870–71

First Steps, after Millet
Vincent van Gogh
Dutch, 1853–1890
Oil on canvas

Dance to Your Daddy

Based on a Scottish dandling rhyme, this song became popular in communities where men were often at sea and women comforted their children and themselves with thoughts of the boats' return.

Madame Roulin and Her Baby
Vincent van Gogh
Dutch, 1853–1890
Oil on canvas

Now the Day Is Over

This gentle hymn evokes the calm that settles over the land, and the household, as night descends. Lyrics by the Reverend Sabine Baring-Gould (1834–1924) were set to music by Sir Joseph Barnby (1838–1896).

A Domestic Scene
Annibale Carracci
Italian, 1560–1609
Pen and black ink, gray and brown wash; early 1580s

12

Peacefully

Now the day is o - ver, Night is draw-ing nigh,

Sha - dows of the eve - ning Steal a - cross the sky.

Gobelle's Mill at Optevoz
Charles-François Daubigny
French, 1817–1878
Oil on canvas

All the Pretty Little Horses

Originating in the American South, this lullaby has a haunting melody that soothes a child to sleep while its imagery inspires sweet dreams.

Restfully

Hush - a - bye,   don't you cry,   Go to sleep-y, lit - tle   ba - by.

When you wake,   you shall have   All the pret-ty lit-tle   hors - es.

Blacks and bays,   dap-ples and grays,   Coach and six __ white __   hors - es.

Hush - a - bye,   don't you cry,   Go to sleep-y, lit - tle   ba - by.

(Please turn the page.)

Robert Wade Young, Young Boy with Cock Horse
Augustin Edouart
British (b. France), 1789–1861
Cut-paper silhouette

All the Pretty Little Horses continued

José Costa y Bonnells, Called Pepito
Francisco de Goya
Spanish, 1746–1828
Oil on canvas

Children on a Rocking Horse (detail)
Josef von Divéky
Austrian, 1887–1951
Color lithograph published by the
Wiener Werkstätte, Vienna

When you wake, you shall have cake And all the pret-ty lit-tle hors - es.

Blacks and bays, dap-ples and grays, Coach and six __ white __ hors - es.

Walking beat

Mam - my loves and Pap-py loves, And Mam-my loves _ her ba - by.

Go to sleep-y, go to sleep, Go to sleep, you lit-tle ba - by.

Mammy Loves

Babies love repetition. You can sing this song over and over, changing to the names of grand-parents, brothers and sisters, aunts and uncles, baby-sitters, and everyone else who loves the baby.

Mr. and Mrs. Daniel Otis and Child
Joseph H. Davis, American, 1811–1865
Watercolor, gum arabic, and graphite
on off-white wove paper; 1834

Sleep, Baby, Sleep

A very old German song, "Schlaf, Kindlein Schlaf," this melody has been incorporated into compositions by Brahms and Wagner.

Lamb (detail)
Josef von Divèky
Austrian, 1887–1951
Color lithograph published by the
Wiener Werkstätte, Vienna

Slowly

1. Sleep, ba-by, sleep, Your fa-ther tends the sheep, Your moth-er shakes the
2. Sleep, ba-by, sleep, Our cot-tage vale is deep, The lit-tle lamb is

dream-land tree, And sleep, ba-by,
on the green, With snow-y fleece so soft and clean, Sleep, ba-by,
from it fall sweet dreams for thee, Sleep, ba-by,

Pastoral Scene
Detail of needlework upholstery
on the back of an easy chair
American (Newport, Rhode Island), 1758
Wool on linen

1.
sleep, Sleep, ba-by, sleep.
sleep,

Last time
Sleep, ba-by, sleep.

Dance, Little Baby

The "merry gay coral" in this nursery rhyme is a kind of rattle common in the eighteenth and nineteenth centuries. The bells jingle and the coral can be used for teething. Since ancient times, coral has been believed to protect children against evil.

Rattle, with Whistle, Coral, and Bells
Nicholas Roosevelt
American (New York), 1715–1769
Gold, coral

Mother and Child
Edward Steichen
American, 1879–1973
Direct carbon print, 1905

(Please turn the page.)

Dance, Little Baby continued

down to the ground, | Back - wards and for - wards, | round and __ round:

Dance, lit - tle ba - by, and | moth-er shall sing, With the | mer-ry gay cor - al, ding,

ding-a-ding, ding; With the | mer-ry gay cor-al, sing | ding - a - ding - a - | ding.

Mother Playing with Children
Utagawa Toyoharu
Japanese, 1735–1806
Color on silk

Brahms' Lullaby

Lul-la - by and good night, With_ ro - ses be - dight,_ With_

lil - ies be - spread, Is_ ba - by's wee bed. Lay thee

down now and rest, May thy slum - ber be blessed. Lay thee

(To be played or sung)

down now and rest, May thy slum - ber be blessed. (Lul - la -

In this well-known lullaby by Johannes Brahms (1833–1897), the roses and lilies decorating baby's bed suggest the purity, innocence, and sweetness of the sleeping child.

Infante Carlos Luis María Fernando de Borbón
Luis de la Cruz y Rios
Spanish, active by 1815, d. 1850
Ivory, 1818

(Please turn the page.)

Brahms' Lullaby continued

Sleeping Eros
Greek, 3rd–2nd century B.C.
Bronze

Child Asleep (The Rosebud)
Thomas Sully
American, 1783–1872
Oil on canvas, 1841

down　　　　now and　rest,　　May thy　slum - ber　be　blessed.)

Armenian Lullaby

With its simple but beautiful melody in a minor key, this song has the feeling of an old, traditional folk tune.

Gently rocking

Sleep, my lit-tle one, my __ loved one,

As I rock and sing, As the bright____

moon watch-es o'er us, O'er your lit - tle crib.

Peasant Mother and Child
Mary Cassatt
American, 1844–1926
Drypoint and aquatint printed in colors,
ca. 1894

Autumn Grasses (detail)
Shibata Zeshin
Japanese, 1807–1891
Panel from a two-fold screen;
ink, lacquer, and silver leaf on paper

Swing Low, Sweet Chariot

The words of this beloved spiritual express the thoughts of someone who is ready to lay down the cares of the world and to take heavenly rest.

Swing low, sweet char - i - ot, __ Com-in' for to car-ry me home.

Swing __ low, sweet char - i - ot, __ Com-in' for to car-ry me home.

1. I looked o - ver Jor - dan and what did I see, __
2. If you get to heav - en be - fore I do, __

Com-in' for to car - ry me home, A band __ of an - gels
Com-in' for to car - ry me home, Tell all __ my friends I'm

com-in' af - ter me, __ Com-in' for to car-ry me home.
com-in' there, too, __ Com-in' for to car-ry me home.

The Block (detail)
Romare Bearden
American, 1911–1988
Cut-and-pasted papers
on Masonite, 1971

Shaker Rocking Chair
American, ca. 1820–50
Maple, birch

29

Can Ye Sew Cushions

The lyrics of this Scottish song seem gloomy, but the mother ("minnie")
is probably worrying about her children ("many o' ye, little for to gi' ye")
and trying to calm a baby who cries ("greets").

Easily

1. Oh, can ye sew cush-ions, and can ye sew sheets, And
2. Now hush - a - ba, lam - mie, and hush - a - ba, dear, Now

can ye sing_ ba - la - loo_ when the bairn greets? And
hush - a - ba,_ lam-mie, thy_ min - nie is here. And

hee and baw bird - ie, and hee and baw lamb, And

Rest and Work
Jean Charlot
Mexican, 1898–1979
Color lithograph on stone, 1945

Monday Morning
B. J. O. Norfeldt
American, 1878–1955
Color woodblock print

(Please turn the page.)

hee and baw bird - ie, my bon - nie wee lamb.

Refrain
Bagpipe tempo

Hee O, wee O, what will I do wi' ye? Black's the life that

I lead wi' ye, Ma - ny o' ye, lit - tle for to gi' ye,

Hee O, wee O, what will I do wi' ye?

Penelope
Charles-François Marchal
French, 1825–1877
Oil on canvas

The Lacemaker
Nicolaes Maes
Dutch, 1634–1693
Oil on canvas

Mozart's Lullaby

Mozart's gentle harmonies seem a perfect accompaniment to these descriptions of nature at twilight.

The First Babe (detail)
Jehan-Georges Vibert
French, 1840–1902
Watercolor, 1872

Grand Piano
Ferdinand Hofmann (d. 1829)
Vienna, ca. 1790
Cherrywood and
other materials

(Please turn the page.)

34

Mozart's Lullaby continued

A Goose Hiding Its Head
Alfred Sisley
British, 1839–1899
Pencil and colored crayon on paper

Mother and Child
Pierre Bonnard
French, 1867–1947
Lithograph; back cover of
Petit Solfège Illustré, 1893

The Sandman

The Sandman has made his way from folklore to popular culture as the benevolent being who sprinkles his sleep-inducing sand into children's eyes.

Midnight: Mother and Sleepy Child
Kitagawa Utamaro
Japanese, 1753–1806
Polychrome woodblock print from
the series *Customs of Women in the Twelve Hours*

Raisins and Almonds

The little goat in this Yiddish lullaby brings almonds and raisins, probably symbolizing the sweetness in life that parents wish for their children.

The Baby
Alice Boughton
American, 1865–1943
Gelatin silver print, 1908

Slowly and easily

To my lit-tle one's cra-dle in the night, _____ Comes a

lit-tle goat snow—y and white; _____ The goat will trot to the

mar-ket, ____ While moth-er her watch_ does keep,

Bring-ing back rai-sins and al-monds. _ Sleep, my lit-tle one, sleep. ___

All Through the Night

Set to a beautiful old Welsh folk tune, these lyrics by
Sir Harold Boulton (1859–1935) reassure children
that they are loved and protected, all through the night.

1. Sleep, my child, and peace at-tend thee, All through the night.
2. While the moon her watch is keep-ing, All through the night;

Rabbit in a Landscape with Moon
Chinese, mid-18th century
Embroidered silk

Guar-dian an-gels God will send thee, All through the night.
While the wea-ry world is sleep-ing, All through the night;

Soft the drow-sy hours are creep-ing, Hill and vale in slum-ber steep-ing,

Jonathan
Eliot Porter
American, 1901–1990
Gelatin silver print, 1938

(Please turn the page.)

I my lov - ing vig - il keep - ing, All through the night.

O'er thy spi - rit gent - ly steal-ing, Vi - sions of de - light re-veal-ing,

Bahram Gur Watching Dilaram Charm
the Wild Animals with Her Music
Page from the *Hasht Behesht*
(Eight Paradises) of Amir Khusrau Dihlavi
Indian, Mughal, probably Lahore,
period of Akbar (r. 1556–1605)
Attributed to Miskin
Ink and opaque watercolor
on paper, ca. 1595

Breathes a pure and ho - ly feel - ing, All through the night.

Mughal Virgin and Child
Indian, Mughal period, 17th century
Brush drawing, black and colored inks
and gold on paper

Golden Slumbers

Set to a seventeenth-century English tune, the lyrics of this lovely song are attributed to Thomas Dekker (1572–1632), the English dramatist. They are perhaps better known as sung by the Beatles.

Sleepily

1. Gol - den slum - bers kiss your eyes,
2. Care __ you know not, there - fore sleep,

Smiles __ a - wait you when you rise.
While __ I o'er you when you watch do keep.

Sleep, pret - ty ba - by, do __ not cry, __ And
Sleep, pret - ty dar - lings, do __ not cry, __ And

Cradle
English, first half of the 17th century
Oak and walnut

The Young Mother
Nicolaes Maes
Dutch, 1634–1693
Pen and brown ink, brown wash

Lizzie at the Table
Fairfield Porter
American, 1907–1975
Oil on canvas, 1958

Skidamarink

*Sing "Skidamarink" to a child waking up in the morning or after a nap,
or any time you want to say "I love you."*

Lively enough

Skid-a-ma-rink a - dink a-dink,   Skid-a-ma-rink a - doo,

I   love   you.

Skid-a-ma-rink a-dink a-dink,   Skid-a-ma-rink a - doo,

I   love   you.   I

(Please turn the page.)

*Two Lovers, Sankatsu and
Hanhichi, with Their Baby*
Kitagawa Utamaro
Japanese, 1753–1806
Polychrome woodblock print

47

Family Scene
Pierre Bonnard
French, 1867–1943
Color lithograph, 1893

love you in the morn-ing and in the af - ter - noon, I

love you in the eve - ning and un - der-neath the moon, Oh,

Skid-a - ma-rink a - dink a-dink, Skid-a - ma-rink a - doo,

I love you. ____

Day Is Done

All the world is at peace and ready to rest at the end of the day.

Very slowly—without a beat

p Day is done, Gone the sun, From the lake, From the hills, From the

sky. All is well, Safe - ly rest. God is nigh.

Hooked Rug
Lucy Barnard
American (Dixfield Common, Maine)
Burlap, yarn, and cloth; ca. 1860

Suo Gan (Lullaby)

*What could be more comforting
to a child than to be wrapped
in Mother's arms, snuggled
against her chest, as described
in this old Welsh song?*

Easily and slowly

mp Sleep, my ba - by, on my bo - som, Warm and co - zy will it prove; Round thee moth - er's arms are fold - ing, In her heart a moth - er's love. There shall no one come to harm thee, Naught shall ev - er break thy rest.

Mother and Child
Mary Cassatt
American, 1844–1926
Pastel on wove paper, mounted on canvas,
1914

Mother and Child
Camille Corot
French, 1796–1875
Oil on wood

Sleep, my dar-ling babe, in qui-et, Sleep on moth-er's gen-tle breast.

By'm Bye

Instead of counting sheep, try counting stars. You can continue
"Stars shining, number, number seven, number eight, number nine"
and so on until your child falls asleep.

Very freely

By'm bye, by'm bye, Stars shin - ing,

With a little movement

1. Num-ber, num-ber one, num-ber two, num-ber three, Good Lord, by'm
2. Num-ber, num-ber four, num-ber five, num-ber six, Good Lord, by'm

bye, by'm bye, Good Lord, by'm bye.

Alice Cushman
George Hewitt Cushman
American, 1814–1876
Watercolor on ivory, ca. 1856

Landscape with Stars (detail)
Henri-Edmond Cross
French, 1856–1910
Watercolor on paper

Rocking

A Czech carol, this song was originally a lullaby to the infant Jesus.

Standing Figure of Mother and Child
Oceania, Melanesia, Irian Jaya, Lake Sentani region, Kabiterau village
Wood, 19th–20th century

Rockingly

Lit - tle ba - by, sweet-ly __ sleep, do not __ weep,
Sleep in __ com - fort, __ slum - ber __ deep. I will rock you,
rock you, rock you, I will rock you, rock you, rock you.
Lit-tle ba-by, sweet-ly __ sleep, Sleep in __ com-fort, __ slum-ber __ deep.

風流七小町
通ひ

歌麿筆

*Young Mother
Nursing Her Baby*
Kitagawa Utamaro
Japanese, 1753–1806
Polychrome woodblock
print, 1790s

Baby's Bed's a Silver Moon

The vivid image of baby "sailing o'er the sea of sleep" is made poignant by the plea, "Only don't forget to come back again to me."

Imaginary Voyage
Richard Teschner, Austrian, 1879–1948
Color lithograph published by the
Wiener Werkstätte, Vienna

Longingly

1. Ba - by's bed's a sil - ver moon,
2. Ba - by's fish - ing for a dream,

Sail - ing o'er the sky,
Fish - ing near and far,

Sail - ing o'er the sea of sleep,
Her line a sil - ver moon - beam is,

While the stars float by.
Her bait a sil - ver star.

To Refrain after each verse

(Please turn the page.)

Mother with Baby and Young Daughter at the Edge of a Pond
Maurice Prendergast
American, 1858–1924
Watercolor on paper
from the *Large Boston Public Garden Sketchbook,* 1895–97

Refrain

Sail, ba - by, sail,

Far a - cross the sea,

On - ly don't for - get to come

Back a - gain to me.

The Fairy Ship
Illustration by Paul Woodroffe from
Nursery Songs by Joseph Moorat
London, ca. 1907

Maternal Caress
Mary Cassatt
American, 1844–1926
Drypoint, aquatint, and soft-ground
etching printed in color; 1890–91

Hand Studies—Child with Doll
Alma Lavenson
American, 1897–1989
Platinum print, 1932

Rock-a-Bye, Baby

The best-known lullaby in the English language, it is also probably the first that children learn themselves, to sing to their dolls, stuffed animals, or siblings.

Blossom Day
Gertrude Käsebier
American, 1852–1934
Platinum print, 1904–1905

Little Boy Blue

Some children can sleep soundly through any amount of commotion. Little Boy Blue of this nursery rhyme was apparently able to continue his nap in spite of the chaos that ensued.

Bluely

Lit - tle Boy Blue, come blow__ your horn, The

sheep's in the mead - ow, the cow's in the corn.

The Grandchildren of Sir William Heathcote (detail)
William Owen
British, 1769–1825
Oil on canvas

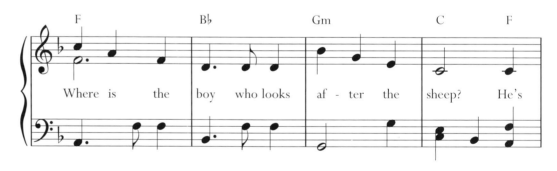

Where is the boy who looks af - ter the sheep? He's

un - der the hay - stack, fast a - sleep.

The Monet Family in Their Garden at Argenteuil (detail)
Édouard Manet
French, 1832–1883
Oil on canvas

Baloo, Baleerie

"Go away, tiny fairies" insists this Gaelic song.
The "ben" is a small inner room, presumably
where the baby sleeps.

Infant Joy
William Blake
British, 1757–1827
Hand-colored relief etching from
Songs of Innocence, 1789

Ba - loo, ba - leer - ie, ba - loo, ba -

leer - ie, Ba - loo, ba - leer - ie, ba - loo, ba - lee.

1. Gang a - wa', peer - ie fair - ies, Gang a - wa', peer - ie

fair - ies, Gang a - wa', peer-ie fair - ies, Frae oor ben noo.

Flying Away and *The Fairy Queen Takes an Airy Drive*
Richard Doyle
British, 1824–1883
Chromolithographs from *In Fairyland: A Series of Pictures from the Elf-World*
Published in London by Longmans, Green, Reader and Dyer, 1870

*Young Mother
Gazing at Her Child*
Adolphe-William
Bouguereau
French, 1825–1905
Oil on canvas

66

Brezairola (Lullaby)

A folk tune from the Auvergne region of France, this beautiful lullaby expresses the sentiment of many exhausted parents: "Slumber, come quickly!" The lyrics are given in the original dialect, with an English translation following.

Easy lilt

Soun, soun, bè-ni, bè - ni, bè - ni; Soun, soun, bè-ni, bè - ni, doun!

Soun, soun, bè-ni, bè - ni, bè - ni; Soun, soun, bè-ni, d'èn do - con!

1. Lou soun soun bouol pas bè-ni, _____ pè-cai - ré! Lou soun soun bouol
2. At - so lo qu'ès por o - qui, _____ pè-cai - ré! At - so lo qu'ès

2nd time skip to ⊕   1st time skip to 𝄉   Fine

pas bè-ni, Lou nè - ni s'en bouol pas dur-mi! Oh!
por o-qui, Lou né - ni s'en bou - lio dur-mi. Ah!

Shepherd
Detail from *The Nativity*
Antoniazzo Romano (Antonio di Benedetto Aquilio)
Italian (Roman), active by 1452, d. by 1512
Tempera on wood

(Please turn the page.)

Brezairola (Lullaby) continued

Mother and Child
Mary Cassatt
American, 1844–1926
Pastel on wove paper, mounted on canvas;
1914

Woman Standing, Child on Back (detail)
Jean Charlot
Mexican, 1898–1979
Color lithograph on zinc, 1933

Soun, soun, bè - ni, bè - ni, bè - ni; Soun, soun,

bè - ni, bè - ni, doun!
bè - ni o l'è - fon!

Lou soun soun bouol pas bè - ni;

1.
L'è-fen-tou bouol pas dur-mi.

2.
Lou soun soun bouol pas bè - ni.

D.C.

English translation:

Come, slumber, come, come,
Come, slumber, come, please come.
Come, slumber, come, come,
Come, slumber, from where you will.

Slumber does not want to come,
   poor baby.
Slumber does not want to come;
Baby cannot fall asleep. Oh!

Come, come, slumber, come quickly!
Come, come, slumber, come down now!
Slumber does not want to come.
Baby does not want to sleep.

Come, come, slumber, come quickly!
Come, come, come to my
   sweet babe!
Slumber does not want to come.
Baby does not want to sleep.

Come, slumber, come, come,
Come, slumber, come, please come.
Come, slumber, come, come,
Come, slumber, from where you will.

Slumber comes, at last it's here, poor baby.
Slumber comes, at last it's here;
Now the baby will fall asleep. Ah!

Kumbayah

This West Indian song calls out with longing, yet with hope, imploring the Lord to "come by here."

The Goddess Isis with Her Son Horus on Her Lap
Egyptian, Ptolemaic Period (305–30 B.C.)
Blue faience

Drum
African, Republic of the Congo,
Vili or Yombe people, 19th century
Wood, carved and painted glass

Raindrops

The gentle drumming of rain on the roof can have the mesmeric effect of a lullaby.

With a slow, rocking pulse

Rain-drops a-fall-ing from the skies, Tired and sleep-y,

close your eyes. Tired and sleep-y, While the skies are weep-ing,

Weep-ing and sing-ing you their lul-la-bies. Tired and sleep-y,

While the skies are weep-ing, Weep-ing and sing-ing you their lul-la-bies.

Mother's Kiss
Mary Cassatt
American, 1844–1926
Drypoint and aquatint printed in color,
ca. 1890–91

Seidō and Kanda River from Shōhei Bridge
(detail)
Utagawa Hiroshige
Japanese, 1797–1858
Woodblock print in colors from the series
One Hundred Famous Views of Edo, 1857

Sweet and Low

Alfred, Lord Tennyson (1809–1892), Poet Laureate of England, wrote this poem, which recounts the words of a woman longing for her husband to return safely from the sea. The melody is by Sir Joseph Barnby (1838–1896).

Slow waltz

Sweet and low, sweet and low,

Wind of the west- ern sea, _____

Low, low, breathe and blow,

Wind of the west — ern sea! ___

O - ver the rol - ling wa — ters go,

Come from the dy - ing moon,_ and blow,

Baby Monsarrat
Clarence H. White
American, 1871–1925
Platinum print, 1905

(Please turn the page.)

Sweet and Low continued

Family Group
Henry Moore
British, 1898–1986
Bronze, 1944

Blow him a - gain to me;_____

While my lit - tle one, while my

pret - ty one sleeps._____

Additional verse:

2. Sleep and rest, sleep and rest,
   Father will come to thee soon;
   Rest, rest, on mother's breast,
   Father will come to thee soon;
   Father will come to his babe in the nest,
   Silver sails all out of the west
   Under the silver moon;
   Sleep, my little one, sleep, my pretty one, sleep.

The Dock
B. J. O. Norfeldt
American, 1878–1955
Color woodblock print

Two Girls, One Holding a Baby
Édouard Vuillard
French, 1868–1940
Color lithograph

Fais Dodo (Go to Sleep)

Go to sleep, my | sweet lit-tle broth-er, sis-ter, | Go to sleep, and

Fais do - do, Co- | *las mon p'tit frè - re,* | *Fais do - do, t'au-*

1.
you'll have a treat. | 2. you'll have a treat. Ma- | ma makes a cake; it's

ras du lo - lo. | *ras du lo - lo. Ma-* | *man est en haut, qui*

read-y to bake; Pa- | pa's down be-low and he's | mak-ing co-coa.

fait du gâ - teau; Pa- | *pa est en bas, qui fait* | *du cho-co-lat.*

Go to sleep, my | sweet lit-tle broth-er, sis-ter, | Go to sleep, my | sweet lit-tle one.

Fais do - do, Co- | *- las mon p'tit frè - re,* | *Fais do - do, t'au-* | *- ras du lo - lo.*

As you sing this old French song, you can change "brother" to "sister," "nephew," "grandchild," "baby," or whatever name is appropriate.

Fais Dodo, Colas
Maurice Boutet de Monvel
French, 1851–1913
Illustration from *Vieilles chansons et rondes pour les petits enfants*
Published in Paris

79

Toora, Loora, Loora

Though mostly nonsense syllables, this song by James R. Shannon seems to express a longing for the writer's homeland and childhood.

(Please turn the page.)

Family Group
Gertrude Käsebier, American, 1852–1934
Platinum print, 1902

Nurse and Child (detail)
Mary Cassatt, American, 1844–1926
Pastel on colored wove paper, mounted
on canvas; 1897

81

Toora, Loora, Loora continued

A Nanny with Her Charge
Maurice Prendergast
American, 1858–1924
Watercolor on paper from
the *Large Boston Public Garden
Sketchbook,* 1895–97

Bye, Baby Bunting

Although the origin of the word "bunting" is unclear, it has come to mean a baby's snuggly, hooded sleeper or outer wrapper.

Baby's Bassinet
Illustration from *Le Journal de Bébé* by Marie Madeleine Franc-Nohain
Published by Bernard Grasset, Paris, 1914

Gently swinging

Bye,__ ba - by bunt - ing, Dad - dy's gone a - hunt - ing, To

get a lit - tle rab - bit skin, To wrap his ba - by bunt - ing in.

Twinkle, Twinkle, Little Star

These familiar lyrics first appeared in Rhymes
for the Nursery *by Jane and Ann Taylor,
published in England in 1806. They were later
set to a traditional tune to create this beloved
children's song.*

Slow and twinkling

1. Twin-kle, twin-kle, lit-tle star, How I won-der what you are!
2. When the blaz-ing sun is gone, When he noth-ing shines up-on,

Portrait of a Child (Clara B. Fuller)
Lucia Fairchild Fuller
American, 1872–1924
Watercolor on ivory, 1898

Up a-bove the world so high, Like a dia-mond in the sky.
Then you show your lit-tle light, Twin-kle, twin-kle, all the night.

Twin-kle, twin-kle, lit-tle star, How I won-der what you are!
Twin-kle, twin-kle, lit-tle star, How I won-der what you are!

The Way Home
Ludwig Michaelek
Austrian, 1859–1942
Color etching and aquatint, 1901

Additional verses:

3. Then the trav'ler in the dark
   Thanks you for your tiny spark;
   He could not see which way to go,
   If you did not twinkle so.
   Twinkle, twinkle, little star,
   How I wonder what you are!

4. In the dark blue sky you keep,
   Often through my curtains peep,
   For you never shut your eye,
   Till the sun is in the sky,
   Twinkle, twinkle, little star,
   How I wonder what you are!

When at Night I Go to Sleep

Engelbert Humperdinck (1854–1921) based the evening prayer for his opera Hansel and Gretel *on the German version of "Now I Lay Me Down to Sleep." It is closely related to "Matthew, Mark, Luke, and John."*

Calmly

When at night I / go to sleep, / Four-teen an-gels / watch do _ keep; _

Two my head are / guard - ing, / Two my feet are / guid - ing, _

The Archangel Raphael and Tobias
Neri di Bicci
Italian (Florentine), 1419–1491
Tempera on panel

Two are on my / right hand, _ / Two are on my / left hand,

(Please turn the page.)

Ernesta (Child with Nurse) (detail)
Cecilia Beaux
American, 1855–1942
Oil on canvas, 1894

Two who warm-ly cov – er, Two who o'er me hov – er,

Two to whom 'tis giv – en To guide my steps to heav – en.

Crib of the Infant Jesus
South Netherlandish, Brabant,
15th century
Wood, polychromed and gilt,
lead, silver gilt, painted
parchment, and silk embroidery
with seed pearls, gold thread,
and translucent enamels

Matthew, Mark, Luke, and John

A traditional nursery prayer, this verse seems almost a spell or incantation to protect the bed of the sleeping child.

Prayerfully

Mat-thew, Mark, | Luke, and John, | Bless the bed that | I lie on.

Four cor - ners | to my bed, | Four an - gels | round my head;

One to watch and | one to pray, And | two to guide me | through the day.

Waking
Detail from *A Day in a Child's Life*
Hand-colored wood engraving after a
drawing by Kate Greenaway
(British, 1846–1901), 1881

Asleep
Horace Pippin
American, 1888–1946
Oil on canvas board, 1943

All Night, All Day

It's a cheering thought to imagine that angels are watching over our children day and night.

Fan Quilt
United States, ca. 1900
Cotton

With spirit

D   G   D

1. All night, all __ day, An-gels watch-in' o-ver me, my Lord, __
2. When at night I go to sleep, An-gels watch-in' o-ver me, my Lord, __

D   D/A   D/A   A7   D

All night, all __ day, An - gels watch-in' o-ver me.
Pray the Lord my soul to keep, An - gels watch-in' o-ver me.

91

Good Night to You All

A musical family might sing this round to one another at bedtime.

Virgin and Child with the Young
Saint John the Baptist and Angels
François Boucher
French, 1703–1770
Oil on canvas, 1765

To be sung as a round, voices entering at I, II, and III

Good night to you all, And sweet be your sleep. May

an - gels a - round you their si - lent watch keep. Good

night, good night, good night, good night.

INDEX OF SONG TITLES

INDEX OF FIRST LINES

CREDITS

Page 9: Gift of Frederic H. Hatch, 1926   26.97. *Page 10:* Gift of George N. and Helen M. Richard, 1964   64.165.2. *Page 11:* Robert Lehman Collection, 1975   1975.1.231. *Page 12:* Purchase, Mrs. Vincent Astor and Mrs. Charles S. Payson Gifts and Harris Brisbane Dick and Rogers Funds, 1972   1972.133.2. *Page 13:* Bequest of Robert Graham Dun, 1911   11.45.3. *Page 14:* From the Collection of James Stillman, Gift of Dr. Ernest G. Stillman, 1922   22.16.21. *Page 15:* The Glenn Tilley Morse Collection, Bequest of Glenn Tilley Morse, 1950   50.602.565. *Page 16:* top, Gift of Countess Bismarck, 1961   61.259; bottom, Museum Accession, 1943. *Page 17:* Gift of Edgar William and Bernice Chrysler Garbisch, 1972   1972.263.6. *Page 18:* Museum Accession, 1943. *Page 19:* Gift of Mrs. J. Insley Blair, 1950   50.228.3. *Page 20:* Rogers Fund, 1947   47.70. *Page 21:* Alfred Stieglitz Collection, 1933   33.43.27. *Page 22:* Charles Stewart Smith Collection, Gift of Mrs. Charles Stewart Smith, Charles Stewart Smith Jr. and Howard Caswell Smith, in memory of Charles Stewart Smith, 1914   14.76.70f. *Page 23:* Gift of Mrs. John LaPorte Given, 1945   45.110.4. *Page 24:* Rogers Fund, 1943   43.11.4. *Page 25:* Bequest of Francis T. S. Darley, 1914   14.126.6. *Page 26:* The Harry G. C. Packard Collection of Asian Art, Gift of Harry G. C. Packard and Purchase, Fletcher, Rogers, Harris Brisbane Dick and Louis V. Bell Funds, Joseph Pulitzer Bequest and The Annenberg Fund Inc. Gift, 1975   1975.268.137. *Page 27:* H. O. Havemeyer Collection, Bequest of Mrs. H. O. Havemeyer, 1929   29.107.97. *Page 28:* Friends of the American Wing Fund, 1966   66.10.23. *Page 29:* Gift of Mr. and Mrs. Samuel Shore, 1978   1978.61.2. *Page 30:* Gift of Mrs. B. J. O. Norfeldt, 1955   55.634.79. *Page 31:* Gift of the artist, 1960   60.713.40. *Page 32:* Gift of Mrs. Adolf Obrig, in memory of her husband, 1917   17.138.2. *Page 33:* The Friedsam Collection, Bequest of Michael Friedsam, 1931   32.100.5. *Page 34:* Gift of Geraldine C. Herzfeld, in memory of her husband, Monroe Eliot Hemmerdinger, 1984   1984.34. *Page 35:* Catharine Lorillard Wolfe Collection, Bequest of Catharine Lorillard Wolfe, 1887   87.15.8. *Page 36:* top, Robert Lehman Collection, 1975   1975.1.727b; bottom, Mary Martin Fund, 1987   1987.1117. *Page 37:* Rogers Fund, 1922   JP1278. *Page 38:* Alfred Stieglitz Collection, 1933   33.43.235. *Page 39:* Bequest of Scofield Thayer, 1982   1984.433.2. *Page 40:* Alfred Stieglitz Collection, 1949   49.55.287. *Page 41:* Gift of Alice Boney, 1954   54.37.2. *Page 42:* Gift of Alexander Smith Cochran, 1913   13.228.28. *Page 43:* Rogers Fund, 1970   1970.217. *Page 44:* Gift of Mrs. Paul Moore, 1938   38.72. *Page 45:* Rogers Fund, 1947   47.127.3. *Page 46:* Bequest of Arthur M. Bullowa, 1993   1993.406.2. *Page 47:* Rogers Fund, 1919   JP1123. *Page 48:* Rogers Fund, 1922   22.82.1(3). *Page 49:* Sansbury-Mills Fund, 1961   61.47.3. *Page 50:* H. O. Havemeyer Collection, Bequest of Mrs. H. O. Havemeyer, 1929   29.100.50. *Page 51:* H. O. Havemeyer Collection, Gift of Mrs. P. H. B. Frelinghuysen, 1930   30.13. *Page 52:* Robert Lehman Collection, 1975   1975.1.592. *Page 53:* Fletcher Fund, 1937   37.176.3. *Page 54:* The Michael C. Rockefeller Memorial Collection, Bequest of Nelson A. Rockefeller, 1979   1979.206.1440. *Page 55:* H. O. Havemeyer Collection, Bequest of Mrs. H. O. Havemeyer, 1929   JP1671. *Page 56:* Museum Accession, 1943. *Page 57:* Robert Lehman Collection, 1975   1975.1.953. *Page 58:* Gift of Paul J. Sachs, 1916   16.2.5. *Page 59:* Museum Accession, 1984   1984.1056.24. *Page 60:* Stewart S. MacDermott Fund, 1987   1987.1035. *Page 61:* Alfred Stieglitz Collection, 1933   33.43.135. *Page 62:* Gift of the Heathcote Art Foundation, 1986   1986.264.4. *Page 63:* Bequest of Joan Whitney Payson, 1975   1976.201.14. *Page 64:* top, Gift of Lincoln Kirstein, 1970   1970.565.74; bottom, Rogers Fund, 1917   17.10.25. *Page 65:* Gift of Lincoln Kirstein, 1970   1970.565.74. *Page 66:* Bequest of Zene Montgomery Pyle, 1993   1993.402. *Page 67:* Rogers Fund, 1906   06.1214. *Page 68:* H. O. Havemeyer Collection, Bequest of Mrs. H. O. Havemeyer, 1929   29.100.49. *Page 69:* Gift of the artist, 1960   60.713.42. *Page 70:* Purchase, Joseph Pulitzer Bequest, 1955   55.121.5. *Page 71:* The Crosby Brown Collection of Musical Instruments, 1889   89.4.1743. *Page 72:* The Howard Mansfield Collection, Purchase, Rogers Fund, 1936   JP2512. *Page 73:* Gift of Paul J. Sachs, 1916   16.2.10. *Page 74:* Leonard A. Lauder Collection of American Posters, Gift of Leonard A. Lauder, 1984   1984.1202.57. *Page 75:* Alfred Stieglitz Collection, 1933   33.43.316. *Page 76:* Anonymous Gift, in honor of Alfred H. Barr Jr., 1981   1981.488.4. *Page 77:* Gift of Mrs. B. J. O. Norfeldt, 1955   55.634.80. *Page 78:* Harris Brisbane Dick Fund, 1925   25.70.25. *Page 79:* Gift of Mrs. John S. Lamont, 1974   1974.669. *Page 80:* Gift of Mrs. Ralph J. Hines, 1960   60.181. *Page 81:* Alfred Stieglitz Collection, 1933   33.43.370. *Page 82:* Robert Lehman Collection, 1975   1975.1.942. *Page 83:* The Elisha Whittelsey Collection, The Elisha Whittelsey Fund, 1977   1977.588.1. *Page 84:* Rogers Fund, 1914   14.57.3. *Page 85:* Rogers Fund, 1923   23.52.12(4). *Page 86:* Maria DeWitt Jesup Fund, 1965   65.49. *Page 87:* Robert Lehman Collection, 1975   1975.1.71. *Page 88:* Gift of Ruth Blumka, in memory of Leopold Blumka, 1974   1974.121. *Page 89:* Rogers Fund, 1921   21.36.91. *Page 90:* Bequest of Jane Kendall Gingrich, 1982   1982.55.3. *Page 91:* Purchase, Mrs. Roger Brunschwig Gift, 1988   1988.24.1. *Page 92:* Gift of Miss Adelaide Milton de Groot, in memory of the de Groot and Hawley Families, 1966   66.167.